가장 알기 쉽게 배우는

초등

200여 개 필수 단어와 기본문장 수록

이지영어

STEP BY STEP BOOK 1(입문)

가장 알기 쉽게 배우는

초등 이지 영어
STEP BY STEP BOOK 1(입문)

저 자 방정인
발행인 고본화
발 행 반석출판사
2020년 3월 20일 초판 1쇄 인쇄
2020년 3월 25일 초판 1쇄 발행
홈페이지 www.bansok.co.kr
이메일 bansok@bansok.co.kr
블로그 blog.naver.com/bansokbooks

07547 서울시 강서구 양천로 583. B동 1007호
      (서울시 강서구 염창동 240-21번지 우림블루나인 비즈니스센터 B동 1007호)
대표전화 02) 2093-3399 **팩 스** 02) 2093-3393
출 판 부 02) 2093-3395 **영업부** 02) 2093-3396
등록번호 제315-2008-000033호

ISBN 978-89-7172-914-4 (63740)

가장 알기 쉽게 배우는

초등

이지영어

200여 개 필수 단어와 기본 문장 수록

STEP BY STEP **BOOK** 1(입문)

반석출판사
Bansok

머리말

　　국제화 시대를 맞아 외국어 교육의 필요성은 날로 증대되고 있습니다. 특히 영어 교육의 중요성이 강소뇌고 있는 현실입니다.

　　13세 이전의 초등학교 때가 외국어를 쉽게 익힐 수 있는 가장 이상적인 시기입니다. 그 이유는 LAD(Language Acquisition Device) 라고 하는 대뇌 특수언어습득장치가 13세 이전의 모든 어린이들에게 있기 때문입니다. 따라서 조기 영어교육의 필요성은 아무리 강조하여도 지나치지 않습니다. 조기 영어교육의 성패는 올바른 영어교육 프로그램의 선택에 달려 있다고 볼 수 있습니다.

　　『초등 이지 영어 STEP BY STEP BOOK 1』(입문)은 영어를 처음 시작하는 어린이를 위한 입문편으로, 영어단어 200여 개와 기본문장을 그림과 함께 편집하였습니다.

　　『초등 이지 영어 STEP BY STEP BOOK 2』(문형)는 제 1권에서 배운 문장을 기본으로 하여, 더 많은 400여 개의 단어와, 기본문장 200여 개로 확장, 활용할 수 있도록 문형을 중점으로 편집하였습니다.

　　『초등 이지 영어 STEP BY STEP』 시리즈는 모든 문장을 그림과 함께 편집함으로써, 영어단어와 영어문장을 영상으로 기억할 수 있도록 저술하였습니다. 『초등 이지 영어 STEP BY STEP』은 특히 강의하기에 알맞도록 편집하였습니다.

　　『초등 이지 영어 STEP BY STEP』이 초등학교의 영어교육에 밑거름이 되기를 바라는 바입니다.

저자 방정인

목차

A a	A a
B b	B b
C c	C c
D d	D d
E e	E e
F f	F f
G g	G g
H h	H h

I i	I i
J j	J j
K k	K k
L l	L l
M m	M m
N n	N n
O o	O o
P p	P p
Q q	Q q

R r	R r
S s	S s
T t	T t
U u	U u
V v	V v
W w	W w
X x	X x
Y y	Y y
Z z	Z z

THIS IS A BOOK.

| apple | baby | American |

다음 단어의 빈 칸을 채우세요.

apple   baby   American

| a | pple   b | a | by | A | merican

| | pple   b | | by | | merican

A의 발음을 연구해 봅시다.

1. a[æ]: 우리말에서 [애]로 발음됩니다.
   예 cap, hat, piano, ·········

2. a[eɪ]: 우리말에서 [에이]로 발음됩니다.
   예 table, lady, radio, ·········

3. a[ə]: 우리말에서 [어]로 발음됩니다.
   예 banana, elephant, an, ·········

NEW WORDS

a book	**a notebook**	**book**: 책 **notebook**: 공책
a pencil	**a ball pen**	**pencil**: 연필 **ball pen**: 볼펜
a bag	**an eraser**	**bag**: 가방 **eraser**: 지우개

THIS IS A BOOK.

This is a book.

This is a notebook.

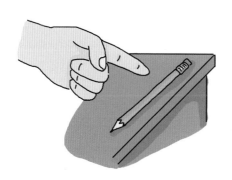

This is a pencil.

This is a ball pen.

This is a bag.

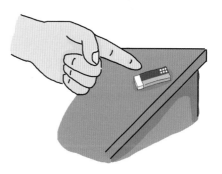

This is an eraser.

★ 다음 그림을 보고 알맞은 단어와 연결하세요.

 •   • book

 •   • eraser

 •   • pencil

 •   • ball pen

 •   • notebook

 •   • bag

12

THAT IS A DESK.

book   **bus**   **umbrella**

다음 단어의 빈 칸을 채우세요.

book   bus   umbrella

$\boxed{b}$ ook $\boxed{b}$ us   um $\boxed{b}$ rella

$\boxed{}$ ook $\boxed{}$ us   um $\boxed{}$ rella

B의 발음을 연구해 봅시다.

1. b[b]: 우리 말에서 [ㅂ]로 발음됩니다.
   예 box, bat, bed, ………

2. b[b]: 우리말에서 [브]로 발음됩니다.
   예 brother, blackboard, breakfast, ………

LESSON 2

13

NEW WORDS

a desk	a chair	**desk**: 책상 **chair**: 의자
a blackboard	a map	**blackboard**: 칠판 **map**: 지도
a picture	a clock	**picture**: 그림, 사진 **clock**: 벽시계

14

THAT IS A DESK.

That is a desk.

That is a chair.

That is a blackboard.

That is a map.

That is a picture.

That is a clock.

★ 다음 그림을 보고 _____친 곳에 알맞은 단어를 써 넣으세요.

 •   • This is a _____.

 •   • This is a _____.

  •   • This is an _____.

 •   • This is a _____.

 •   • This is a _____.

 •   • This is a _____.

IT IS A CAP.

cup   clock   pencil

다음 단어의 빈 칸을 채우세요.

cup	clock	pencil
c up	c lock	pen c il
☐ up	☐ lock	pen ☐ il

C의 발음을 연구해 봅시다.

1. c[k]: 우리말에서 [ㅋ]로 발음됩니다.
   예 cat, car, cow, ………

2. c[k]: 우리말에서 [크]로 발음됩니다.
   예 clock, cry, ………

3. c[s]: 우리말에서 [스]로 발음됩니다.
   예 pencil, face, ice………

a cap	**a hat**	**cap**: 모자 **hat**: 중절모
a watch	**a key**	**watch**: 시계 **key**: 열쇠
a handbag	**an umbrella**	**handbag**: 손가방 **umbrella**: 우산

IT IS A CAP.

It is a cap.

It is a hat.

It is a watch.

It is a key.

It is a handbag.

It is an umbrella.

★ 다음 단어의 뜻을 쓰세요.

1. cap:

2. hat:

3. watch:

4. key:

5. handbag:

6. umbrella:

7. map:

8. picture:

9. blackboard:

10. eraser:

★ 다음 문장을 우리말로 해석하세요.

1. This is a book.

2. This is a notebook.

3. This is a pencil.

4. This is a ball pen.

5. That is a desk.

6. That is a chair.

7. That is a blackboard.

8. It is a cap.

9. It is a watch.

10. It is an umbrella.

LESSON 4 (FOUR)

I AM A STUDENT.

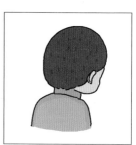

desk   **driver**   **head**

다음 단어의 빈 칸을 채우세요.

desk   driver   head

d esk   d river   hea d

☐ esk   ☐ river   hea ☐

D의 발음을 연구해 봅시다.

1. d[d]: 우리말에서 [ㄷ]로 발음됩니다.
   예 <u>d</u>og, <u>d</u>ish, <u>d</u>esk, ……

2. d[d]: 우리말에서 [드]로 발음됩니다.
   예 <u>d</u>rum, han<u>d</u>, hea<u>d</u>, ………

LESSON 4

21

a student	**a teacher**	**student**: 학생 **teacher**: 선생
a doctor	**a nurse**	**doctor**: 의사 **nurse**: 간호사
a farmer	**a policeman**	**farmer**: 농부 **policeman**: 경찰관

I AM A STUDENT.

I am a student.

I am a teacher.

I am a doctor.

I am a nurse.

I am a farmer.

I am a policeman.

★ 다음 _____ 친 곳에 a나 an을 써 넣으세요. 필요 없는 곳에는 x 표를 하세요.

1. I am _____ student.

2. This is _____ eraser.

3. This is _____ Tom.

4. This is _____ umbrella.

5. It is _____ pencil.

★ 다음 단어의 뜻을 영어로 쓰세요.

1. 책상: 6. 책:

2. 의자: 7. 공책:

3. 칠판: 8. 연필:

4. 그림: 9. 가방:

5. 지도: 10. 지우개:

★ 다음 문장을 우리말로 해석하세요.

1. I am a student.

2. I am a teacher.

3. I am a doctor.

4. I am a nurse.

5. I am a farmer.

YOU ARE A MAN.

| tennis | student | table |

다음 단어의 빈 칸을 채우세요.

tennis	student	table
t e nnis	stud e nt	tabl e
t ☐ nnis	stud ☐ nt	tabl ☐

E의 발음을 연구해 봅시다.

1. e[e]: 우리말에서 [에]로 발음됩니다.
   예 desk, bed, ten, ………

2. e[ə]: 우리말에서 [어]로 발음됩니다.
   예 student, camera, father, ………

3. e[ ]: 우리말에서 발음이 되지 않습니다.
   예 rose, come, write, ………

NEW WORDS

a man	**a woman**	**man**: 남자, 사람 **woman**: 여자
a gentleman	**a lady**	**gentleman**: 신사 **lady**: 숙녀
a child	**a baby**	**child**: 아이 **baby**: 아기

You are a man.

You are a woman.

You are a gentleman.

You are a lady.

You are a child.

You are a baby.

LESSON 5

★ 다음 단어의 뜻을 쓰세요.

1. student: 6. man:

2. teacher: 7. woman:

3. doctor: 8. gentleman:

4. nurse: 9. lady:

5. farmer: 10. child:

★ 다음 문장을 해석하세요.

1. You are a man.

2. You are a woman.

3. You are a gentleman.

4. You are a lady.

5. You are a child.

6. You are a baby.

7. I am a policeman.

8. This is a bag.

9. That is a clock.

10. It is a key.

HE IS TOM.

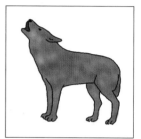

father   **floor**   **wolf**

다음 단어의 빈 칸을 채우세요.

father   floor   wolf

| f | ather | f | loor   wol | f |

☐ ather   ☐ loor   wol ☐

F의 발음을 연구해 봅시다.

1. f[f]: 우리말에서 [ㅍ]로 발음됩니다.
   예 five, fox, farmer, ………

2. f[f]: 우리말에서 [프]로 발음됩니다.
   예 flower, wolf, after, ………

NEW WORDS

Tom	a boy	**Tom**: 탐 **boy**: 소년
a schoolboy	Jane	**schoolboy**: 남학생 **Jane**: 제인
a girl	a schoolgirl	**girl**: 소녀 **schoolgirl**: 여학생

He is Tom.

He is a boy.

He is a schoolboy.

She is Jane.

She is a girl.

She is a schoolgirl.

LESSON 6

★ 다음 ( ) 안에서 알맞은 be 동사를 고르세요.

1. This (am, are, is) a book.

2. That (am, are, is) an eraser.

3. It (am, are, is) a student.

4. I (am, are, is) a student.

5. You (am, are, is) a teacher.

6. He (am, are, is) a nurse.

7. This (am, are, is) Tom.

8. That (am, are, is) Jane.

9. I (am, are, is) a policeman.

10. You (am, are, is) a doctor.

11. He (am, are, is) a boy.

12. She (am, are, is) a girl.

13. Tom (am, are, is) a schoolboy.

14. Jane (am, are, is) a schoolgirl.

15. He (am, are, is) a gentleman.

16. She (am, are, is) a lady.

17. This (am, are, is) an umbrella.

18. That (am, are, is) a table.

19. It (am, are, is) a picture.

20. I (am, are, is) a driver.

IS THIS A RADIO?

G

garden   **glove**   **bag**

다음 단어의 빈 칸을 채우세요.

garden   glove   bag

g arden   g love   ba g

☐ arden   ☐ love   ba ☐

G의 발음을 연구해 봅시다.

1. g[g]: 우리말에서 [ㄱ]로 발음됩니다.
   예 game, guitar, good, ………

2. g[g]: 우리말에서 [그]로 발음됩니다.
   예 glove, Greece, grandfather, ………

3. g[g]: 우리말에서 [그]로 발음됩니다.
   예 dog, bag, ………

NEW WORDS

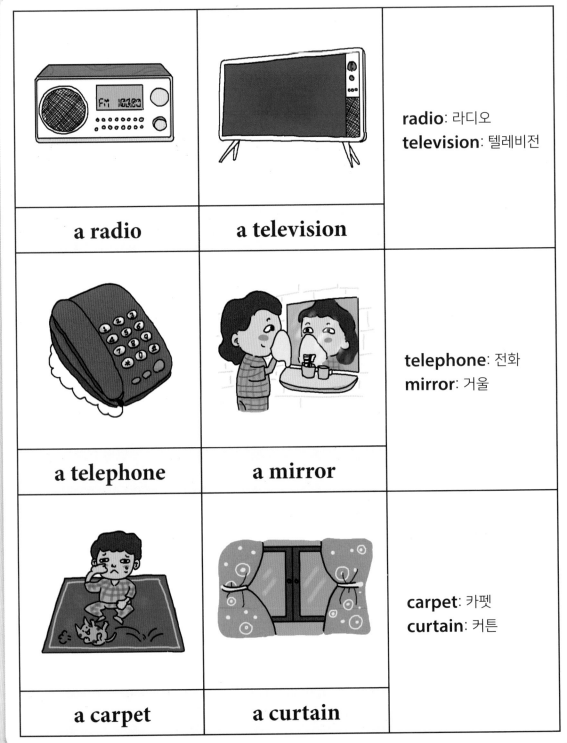

a radio	a television	**radio**: 라디오 **television**: 텔레비전
a telephone	a mirror	**telephone**: 전화 **mirror**: 거울
a carpet	a curtain	**carpet**: 카펫 **curtain**: 커튼

IS THIS A RADIO?

Is this a radio?
Yes, it is.

Is this a television?
Yes, it is.

Is this a telephone?
Yes, it is a telephone.

Is that a mirror?
Yes, it is.

Is that a carpet?
Yes, it is.

Is that a curtain?
Yes, it is a curtain.

★ 다음 <보기> 처럼 의문문으로 만드세요.

 보기 This is a book.
         Is this a book?

1. This is a radio.
2. This is a television.
3. This is a telephone.
4. That is a carpet.
5. That is a curtain.

★ 다음 <보기> 처럼 두 사람의 대화에서 _____친 곳에 알맞은 말을 써 넣으세요.

 보기 Is this a book?
         Yes, it is.
Is this a book?
         Yes, it is a book.

1. Is this a notebook?

   Yes, _____ is.

2. Is this an eraser?

   Yes, _____ is _____ _____ .

3. Is that a mirror?

   Yes, _____ is.

4. Is that a window?

   Yes, _____ is _____ _____ .

LESSON 8(EIGHT)

IS THIS A DOG?

 H

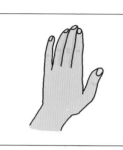

hand

chick

father

다음 단어의 빈 칸을 채우세요.

hand   chick   father

h and   c h ick   fat h er

☐ and   c ☐ ick   fat ☐ er

H의 발음을 연구해 봅시다.

1. h[h]: 우리말에서 [ㅎ]로 발음됩니다.
   예 <u>h</u>at, <u>h</u>ouse, <u>h</u>air, ·········

2. ch[ʧ]: c와 h가 같이 쓰여 우리말에서 [취]로 발음됩니다.
   예 wat<u>ch</u>, <u>ch</u>air, <u>ch</u>ild, ·········

3. th[ð]: t와 h가 같이 쓰여 우리말에서 [드]로 발음됩니다.
   예 mo<u>th</u>er, <u>th</u>is, bro<u>th</u>er, ·········

LESSON 8

a dog	a cat	**dog**: 개 **cat**: 고양이
a hen	a chick	**hen**: 암탉 **chick**: 병아리
a cow	a horse	**cow**: 암소 **horse**: 말

IS THIS A DOG?

Is this a dog?
No, it isn't.

Is this a cat?
No, it isn't.

Is this a hen?
No, it isn't. It's a chick.

Is that a cow?
No, it isn't.

Is that a horse?
No, it isn't.

Is that a pencil?
No, it isn't. It's a ball pen.

★ 다음<보기>처럼 두 사람의 대화에서 _____친 곳에 알맞은 말을 써 넣으세요.

> **보기**
>
> Is this a book?
>> No, it isn't.
>
> Is this a book?
>> No, it isn't a book.

1. Is this a dog?

   No, it _____.

2. Is this a cat?

   No, it _____ ___ _____.

3. Is that a hen?

   No, it _____ _____ _____.

4. Is that a cow?

   No, it _____.

5. Is that a pencil?

   No, it _____. _____ ____ ball pen.

★ 다음 문장을 우리말로 해석하세요.

1. Is this a radio?

   Yes, it is.

2. Is this a television?

   Yes, it is a television.

3. Is that a curtain?

   Yes, it is.

ARE YOU MR. BROWN?

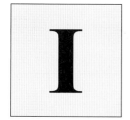

fish	kind	girl

다음 단어의 빈 칸을 채우세요.

fish   kind   girl

f [i] sh   k [i] nd   g [i] rl

f [ ] sh   k [ ] nd   g [ ] rl

I의 발음을 연구해 봅시다.

1. i[i]: 우리말에서 [이]로 발음됩니다.
   예 sister, piano, kitchen, ………

2. i[aɪ]: 우리말에서 [아이]로 발음됩니다.
   예 child, high, smile, ………

3. i[ə]: 우리말에서 [어-]로 발음됩니다.
   예 bird, first, birthday, ………

NEW WORDS

Mr. Brown	Miss Brown	**Mr. Brown**: 브라운씨 **Miss Brown**: 브라운 양
Korean	Chinese	**Korean**: 한국인, 한국어 **Chinese**: 중국인, 중국어
American	English	**American**: 미국인, 미국의 **English**: 영국인, 영어

ARE YOU MR.BROWN?

Are you Mr. Brown?
Yes, I am.

Are you Miss Brown?
Yes, I am Miss Brown.

Is she Korean?
Yes, she is.

Is he Chinese?
Yes, he is Chinese.

Is he American?
Yes, he is.

Is he English?
Yes, he is English.

★ 다음 <보기>처럼 두 사람의 대화에서 _____친 곳에 알맞은 말을 써 넣으세요.

> **보기**
> Are you a student?
>   Yes, I am.
> Are you a student?
>   Yes, I am a student.

1. Are you Mr. Brown?

   Yes, _____ am.

2. Are you Miss Brown?

   Yes, _____ am _____ _____.

3. Is she Korean?

   Yes, _____ is.

4. Is he American?

   Yes, _____ is.

5. Is he English?

   Yes, _____ is _____.

★ 다음 문장을 해석하세요.

1. Is this a dog?

   No, it isn't.

2. Is this a cat?

   No, it isn't a cat.

3. Is that a pencil?

   No, it isn't a pencil. It's a ball pen.

ARE YOU HIS FATHER?

J

jacket   jam   jump

 다음 단어의 빈 칸을 채우세요.

jacket   jam   jump

| j | acket | j | am | j | ump

| ☐ | acket | ☐ | am | ☐ | ump

 J의 발음을 연구해 봅시다.

1. j[ʤ]: 우리말에서 [쥐]로 발음됩니다.
   예 John, June,………

LESSON 10

NEW WORDS

a father	a mother	**father**: 아버지 **mother**: 어머니
a brother	a sister	**brother**: 형제, 남동생 **sister**: 자매, 누이
a son	a daughter	**son**: 아들 **daughter**: 딸

ARE YOU HIS FATHER?

Are you his father?
No, I'm not.

Are you his mother?
No, I'm not. I'm her mother.

Is he your brother?
No, he isn't.

Is he your son?
No, he's not. He's her son.

LESSON 10

Is she your sister?
No, she isn't.

Is she your daughter?
No, she's not.
She's his daughter.

★ 다음 <보기>처럼 두 사람의 대화에서 _____친 곳에 알맞은 말을 써 넣으세요.

보기 Are you American?
          No, I'm not.
       Are you American?
          No, I'm not. I'm English.

1. Are you his father?

   No, _____ _____.

2. Are you his mother?

   No, _____ _____. _____ her mother.

3. Is he your brother?

   No, _____ _____.

4. Is he your son?

   No, _____ _____. _____ her son.

5. Is she your sister?

   No, _____ _____.

★ 다음 ( )안의 단어를 옳게 고쳐 _____친 곳에 써 넣으세요.

1. I am _____brother. ....(you)

2. You are _____ father. ....(he)

3. He is _____ uncle. ....(you)

4. He is _____ brother. ....(she)

5. Jane is _____ sister. ....(Tom)

IS THIS AN APPLE OR AN ORANGE?

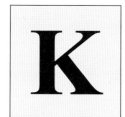

king   **notebook**   **knife**

다음 단어의 빈 칸을 채우세요.

king	notebook	knife
k ing	noteboo k	k nife
☐ ing	noteboo ☐	☐ nife

K의 발음을 연구해 봅시다.

1. k[k]: 우리말에서 [ㅋ]로 발음됩니다.
   예 key, kite, Korean , ·········

2. k[k]: 우리말에서 [ㅋ]로 발음됩니다.
   예 notebook, walk, look, ·········

3. k[ ]: 발음되지 않습니다.
   예 knife, know, knight, ·········

NEW WORDS

		apple: 사과 orange: 오렌지
an apple	**an orange**	
		lemon: 레몬 banana: 바나나
a lemon	**a banana**	
		melon: 멜론 strawberry: 딸기
a melon	**a strawberry**	

IS THIS AN APPLE OR AN ORANGE?

Is this an apple or an orange?
It is an apple.

Is this a lemon or a banana?
It is a banana.

Is this a melon or a strawberry?
It is a melon.

Is that a hen or a chick?
It is a chick.

Is that a map or a picture?
It is a picture.

Is that a watch or a clock?
It is a watch.

★ 다음 문장을 해석하세요.

1. Is this an apple or an orange?

   It is an apple.

2. Is this a lemon or a banana?

   It is a banana.

3. Is this a melon or a strawberry?

   It is a melon.

4. Is that a map or a picture?

   It is a picture.

5. Is that a hen or a chick?

   It is a chick.

★ 다음 단어의 뜻을 쓰세요.

1. dog :

2. cat :

3. hen :

4. chick :

5. horse :

6. cow :

7. brother :

8. sister :

9. son :

10. daughter :

WHAT IS THIS?

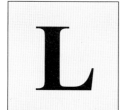

lady　　　　**cloud**　　　　**ball**

다음 단어의 빈 칸을 채우세요.

lady　　　　　　cloud　　　　　ball

$\boxed{l}$ ady　　　c $\boxed{l}$ oud　　　ba $\boxed{l}$ $\boxed{l}$

$\boxed{}$ ady　　　c $\boxed{}$ oud　　　ba $\boxed{}$ $\boxed{}$

l의 발음을 연구해 봅시다.

1. l[l]: 우리말에서 [ㄹ]로 발음됩니다.
   예 lamp, lake, leaf, ………
   close, cloud, playground,…………

2. l[l]: 우리말에서 [ㄹ]로 발음됩니다.
   예 baseball, tall, all, ………

NEW WORDS

		rabbit: 토끼 **mouse**: 생쥐
a rabbit	**a mouse**	
		lion: 사자 **tiger**: 호랑이
a lion	**a tiger**	
		fox: 여우 **wolf**: 늑대
a fox	**a wolf**	

WHAT IS THIS?

What is this?
It is a rabbit.

What is this?
It is a mouse.

What's this?
It's a lion.

What is that?
It is a tiger.

What is that?
It is a fox.

What's that?
It's a wolf.

★ 다음 그림을 보고 질문에 알맞은 말을 _____친 곳에 써 넣으세요.

What is this?
It is a _____.

What is this?
It is a _____.

What is this?
It is a _____.

What is that?
It is a _____.

What is that?
It is a _____.

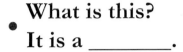

What is that?
It is a _____.

ARE YOU A FARMER OR AN ENGINEER?

Mom **umbrella** **album**

다음 단어의 빈 칸을 채우세요.

Mom   umbrella   album

M om   u m brella   albu m

☐ om   u ☐ brella   albu ☐

M의 발음을 연구해 봅시다.

1. m[m]: 우리말에서 [ㅁ]로 발음됩니다.
   예 <u>m</u>other, <u>m</u>outh, <u>m</u>an, ………
       wo<u>m</u>an, s<u>m</u>ile, le<u>m</u>on, ………

2. m[m]: 우리말에서 [ㅁ]로 발음됩니다.
   예 roo<u>m</u>, ar<u>m</u>, To<u>m</u>, …………

LESSON 13

an engineer	**a mailman**	**engineer**: 기술자 **mailman**: 우체부
a scientist	**a fisherman**	**scientist**: 과학자 **fisherman**: 어부
a pianist	**a cook**	**pianist**: 피아니스트 **cook**: 요리사

ARE YOU A FARMER OR AN ENGINEER?

Are you a farmer or an engineer?
I'm an engineer.

Are you a mailman or a teacher?
I'm a mailman.

Is he a scientist or a doctor?
He's a scientist.

Is he a farmer or a fisherman?
He's a fisherman.

Is she a pianist or a nurse?
She's a pianist.

Is she a doctor or a cook?
She's a cook.

★ 다음 문장을 해석하세요.

1. Are you Korean?
   Yes, I am.

2. Are you American?
   No, I'm not. I'm English.

3. What's this?
   It's a lion.

4. What's that?
   It's a tiger.

5. What's your father?
   He's an engineer.

6. Are you a mailman or a teacher?
   I'm a mailman.

7. Is he a scientist or a doctor?
   He's a scientist.

8. Is she a pianist or a nurse?
   She's a pianist.

WHO ARE YOU?

 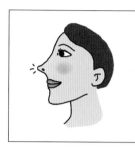  

| nose | winter | violin |

다음 단어의 빈 칸을 채우세요.

| nose | winter | violin |

| n ose | wi n ter | violi n |

| ☐ ose | wi ☐ ter | violi ☐ |

N의 발음을 연구해 봅시다.

1. n[n]: 우리말에서 [ㄴ]로 발음됩니다.
   예 notebook, nine, nurse, ········

2. n[n]: 우리말에서 [ㄴ]로 발음됩니다.
   예 pencil, finger, handbag, ········
   kitchen, spoon, open, ········

who	**Jack**	**who**: 누구 **Jack**: 잭(남자이름)
a friend	**Judy**	**friend**: 친구 **Judy**: 쥬디(여자이름)
an uncle	**an aunt**	**uncle**: 아저씨, 삼촌 **aunt**: 아주머니, 이모

WHO ARE YOU?

Who are you?
I'm Jack.

Who are you?
I'm Jack's friend.

Who is he?
He's Mr. Brown.

Who is he?
He's Tom's uncle.

Who is she?
She's Judy.

Who is she?
She's Judy's aunt.

★ 다음 문장을 해석하세요.

1. Who are you?

   I'm Jack.

2. Who are you?

   I'm Jack's friend.

3. Who is he?

   He's Mr. Brown.

4. Who is he?

   He's Tom's uncle.

5. Who is she?

   She's Judy's aunt.

★ 다음 단어의 뜻을 쓰세요.

1. cook :   6. her :

2. fisherman :   7. what :

3. my :   8. who :

4. your :   9. or :

5. his :   10. Tom's :

WHERE IS YOUR FATHER?

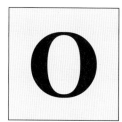

old　　　**cow**　　　**hot**

다음 단어의 빈 칸을 채우세요.

old　　　　　cow　　　　　hot

o ld　　　　c o w　　　　h o t

ld　　　　c w　　　　h t

O의 발음을 연구해 봅시다.

1. o[oʊ]: 우리말에서 [오우]로 발음됩니다.
   예 open, only, rose, ………

2. o[aʊ]: 우리말에서 [아우]로 발음됩니다.
   예 how, hour, down, ………

3. o[a]: 우리말에서 [아]로 발음됩니다.
   예 Tom, doctor, fox, ………

4. o[ʌ]: 우리말에서 [어]로 발음됩니다.
   예 mother, son, brother, ………

NEW WORDS

		living room: 거실 **kitchen**: 부엌
a living room	**a kitchen**	
		garden: 정원 **dining room**: 식당
a garden	**a dining room**	
		bedroom: 침실 **bathroom**: 욕실, 화장실
a bedroom	**a bathroom**	

WHERE IS YOUR FATHER?

Where is your father?
He is in the living room.

Where is your mother?
She is in the kitchen.

Where is your brother?
He's in the garden.

Where is your sister?
She's in the dining room.

Where is your son?
He's in the bedroom.

Where is your daughter?
She's in the bathroom.

★ 다음 두 사람의 대화에서 ＿＿친 곳에 알맞은 말을 써 넣으세요.

1. _____ is this?

   It is a rabbit.

2. _____ is she?

   She is a nurse.

3. _____ is he?

   He is Tom.

4. _____ is she?

   She is my sister.

5. _____ is he?

   He is in the living room.

6. _____ is your mother?

   She is in the kitchen.

7. _____ is that?

   It is a mouse.

8. Is this a book _____ a notebook?

   It is a book.

★ 다음 단어의 뜻을 쓰세요.

1. living room :   6. bathroom :

2. kitchen :   7. cook :

3. garden :   8. apple :

4. dining room :   9. orange :

5. bedroom :   10. strawberry :

I AM TALL.

pen   present   cup

다음 단어의 빈 칸을 채우세요.

pen   present   cup

p en   p resent   cu p

☐ en   ☐ resent   cu ☐

P의 발음을 연구해 봅시다.

1. p[p]: 우리말에서 [ㅍ]로 발음됩니다.
   예 pencil, pin, party, ·········

2. p[p]: 우리말에서 [프]로 발음됩니다.
   예 play, please, pretty, ·········

3. p[p]: 우리말에서 [ㅍ]로 발음되고 받침으로 쓰입니다.
   예 cap, map, jump, ·········

LESSON 16

tall	short	**tall**: 키가 큰 **short**: 키가 작은
handsome	pretty	**handsome**: 잘 생긴 **pretty**: 예쁜
big	little	**big**: 큰 **little**: 작은

I am tall.

You are short.

He is handsome.

She is pretty.

The lion is big.

The mouse is little.

★ 다음 문장을 영어로 쓰세요.

1. 나는 학생입니다.

2. 나는 키가 큽니다.

3. 당신은 선생님입니다.

4. 당신은 키가 작습니다.

5. 그는 의사입니다.

6. 그는 미남입니다.

7. 그녀는 간호사입니다.

8. 그녀는 예쁩니다.

9. 이것은 사자입니다.

10. 이 사자는 큽니다.

I AM A GOOD STUDENT.

quickly　　　**queen**　　　**quiet**

다음 단어의 빈 칸을 채우세요.

quickly　　　　　queen　　　　　quiet

q uickly　　　　q ueen　　　　q uiet

⬚ uickly　　　　⬚ ueen　　　　⬚ uiet

Q의 발음을 연구해 봅시다.

1. q[kw]: 우리말에서 [쿠]로 발음됩니다.
   예 quarter, quite, quick, ………
   　　squire, ………

good	**kind**	**good**: 좋은 **kind**: 친절한
old	**young**	**old**: 나이가 많은 **young**: 젊은
high	**low**	**high**: 높은 **low**: 낮은

I AM A GOOD STUDENT.

I am a good student.

You are a kind teacher.

He is an old man.

She is a young lady.

This is a high mountain.

That is a low mountain.

★ 다음 문장을 해석하세요.

1. I am tall.

   I am a tall student.

2. You are kind.

   You are a kind boy.

3. He is old.

   He is an old man.

4. She is pretty.

   She is a pretty girl.

5. This lion is big.

   This is a big lion.

6. That mouse is little.

   That is a little mouse.

7. Your sister is young.

   Your sister is a young lady.

8. Your brother is handsome.

   Your brother is a handsome boy.

I HAVE A TOY.

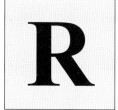   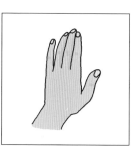

radio　　　**driver**　　　**finger**

다음 단어의 빈 칸을 채우세요.

radio　　　　　driver　　　　　finger

| r | adio　　　d | r | iver　　　finge | r |

☐ adio　　　d ☐ iver　　　finge ☐

R의 발음을 연구해 봅시다.

1. r[r]: 우리말에서 [ㄹ]로 발음됩니다.
   예 rose, rabbit, river, ………

2. r[r]: 우리말에서 [ㄹ]로 발음됩니다.
   예 orange, curtain, airplane, ………

3. r[r]: 우리말에서 [ㄹ]로 발음됩니다.
   예 father, chair, doctor, ………

LESSON 18

a toy	**a ball**	**toy**: 장난감 **ball**: 공
a kite	**a model airplane**	**kite**: 연 **model airplane**: 모형 비행기
a bicycle	**an album**	**bicycle**: 자전거 **album**: 앨범

I HAVE A TOY.

I have a toy.

I have a ball.

You have a kite.

You have a model airplane.

He has a bicycle.

She has an album.

★ 다음 (   ) 안에서 알맞은 말을 고르세요.

1. I (have, has) a toy.

2. You (have, has) a ball.

3. He (have, has) a bicycle.

4. She (have, has) an album.

5. My father (have, has) a car.

6. Your mother (have, has) a handbag.

7. His sister (have, has) a pretty friend.

8. Her brother (have, has) a good friend.

9. Tom's friend (have, has) many books.

10. Mr. Brown's son (have, has) a big kite.

★ 다음 단어의 뜻을 쓰세요.

1. toy :   6. album :

2. ball :   7. good :

3. kite :   8. kind :

4. model airplane :   9. high :

5. bicycle :   10. low :

I PLAY BASEBALL.

 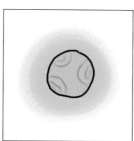  

sun   **skate**   **rose**

다음 단어의 빈 칸을 채우세요.

sun   skate   rose

| s | un | s | kate   ro | s | e

| | un | | kate   ro | | e

S의 발음을 연구해 봅시다.

1. s[s]: 우리말에서 [씨]로 발음됩니다.
   예 son, sister, seven, ·········

2. s[s]: 우리말에서 [스]로 발음됩니다.
   예 school, snow, small, ·········

3. s[z]: 우리말에서 [즈]로 발음됩니다.
   예 please, music, yours, ·········

baseball	**piano**	**baseball**: 야구 **piano**: 피아노
basketball	**violin**	**basketball**: 농구 **violin**: 바이올린
tennis	**organ**	**tennis**: 테니스(정구) **organ**: 풍금

I PLAY BASEBALL.

I play baseball.

I play the piano.

You play basketball.

You play the violin.

He plays tennis.

She plays the organ.

★ 다음 ( )안에서 알맞은 말을 고르세요.

1. I (play, plays) baseball.

2. You (play, plays) basketball.

3. He (play, plays) tennis.

4. She (play, plays) the organ.

5. I (play, plays) the piano.

6. You (play, plays) the violin.

7. He (play, plays) football.

8. Your father (play, plays) golf.

9. Your mother (play, plays) the piano.

★ 다음 단어의 뜻을 쓰세요.

1. baseball :

2. basketball :

3. tennis :

4. piano :

5. violin :

6. organ :

7. play :

8. old :

9. young :

10. tall :

LESSON 20(TWENTY)

DO YOU HAVE A CAR?

| table | truck | hot |

다음 단어의 빈 칸을 채우세요.

table   truck   hot

| t | able | t | ruck   ho | t |

| | able | | ruck   ho | |

T의 발음을 연구해 봅시다.

1. t[t]: 우리말에서 [ㅌ]로 발음됩니다.
   예 tennis, tall, today, ·········

2. t[t]: 우리말에서 [트]로 발음됩니다.
   예 tree, elephant, strawberry, ·········

3. t[t]: 우리말에서 [ㅌ]로 발음됩니다.
   예 but, eat, football, ·········

LESSON 20

		car: 자동차 **motorcycle**: 오토바이
a car	**a motorcycle**	
		knife: 칼 **dish**: 접시
a knife	**a dish**	
		cup: 컵 **glass**: 유리잔
a cup	**a glass**	

Do you have a car?
Yes, I do.

Do you have a
motorcycle?
Yes, I have a motorcycle.

Does he have a knife?
Yes, he does.

Does he have a dish?
Yes, he has a dish.

Does she have a cup?
Yes, she does.

Does she have a glass?
Yes, she has a glass.

★ 다음 <보기>처럼 두 사람의 대화에서 _____친 곳에 알맞은 말을 써 넣으세요.

> **보기**
> Do you have a book?
>   Yes, I do.
> Do you have a book?
>   Yes, I have a book.

1. Do you have a car?

   Yes, I _____.

2. Do you have a motorcycle?

   Yes, I _____ ____ _____.

3. Does he have a knife?

   Yes, he _____.

4. Does he have a dish?

   Yes, he _____.

5. Does she have a cup?

   Yes, she _____.

★ 다음 단어의 뜻을 쓰세요.

1. car :

2. motorcycle :

3. knife :

4. dish :

5. cup :

6. glass :

7. short :

8. handsome :

9. pretty :

10. big :

DO YOU HAVE A BAT?

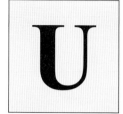   

umbrella　　　　uncle　　　　uniform

다음 단어의 빈 칸을 채우세요.

umbrella　　　　　　uncle　　　　　　uniform

u mbrella　　　　u ncle　　　　u niform

☐ mbrella　　　　☐ ncle　　　　☐ niform

U의 발음을 연구해 봅시다.

1. u[ʌ]: 우리말에서 [어]로 발음됩니다.
   예 under, but, up, ………

2. u[j]: 우리말에서 [유]로 발음됩니다.
   예 use, university, united, ………

		bat: 야구방망이 **glove**: 장갑
a bat	**a glove**	
		doll: 인형 **toy car**: 장난감 차
a doll	**a toy car**	
		flute: 플루트 **guitar**: 기타
a flute	**a guitar**	

DO YOU HAVE A BAT?

Do you have a bat?
No, I don't.

Do you have a glove?
No, I don't have a glove.

Does he have a doll?
No, he doesn't.

Does he have a toy car?
No, he doesn't have a toy car.

Does she have a flute?
No, she doesn't.

Does she have a guitar?
No, she doesn't have a guitar.

★ 다음 <보기>처럼 두 사람의 대화에서 _____친 곳에 알맞은 말을 써 넣으세요.

> **보기**
>
> Do you have a book?
>   No, I don't.
> Do you have a book?
>   No, I don't have a book.

1. Do you have a bat?

   No, I _____.

2. Do you have a glove?

   No, I _____ _____ ___ _____.

3. Does he have a doll?

   No, he _____.

4. Does he have a toy car?

   No, he _____ _____ _____ _____ _____.

5. Does she have a guitar?

   No, she _____.

★ 다음 문장을 해석하세요.

1. Do you have a bat?

   Yes, I do.

2. Do you have a glove?

   Yes, I have a glove.

3. Does he have a doll?

   Yes, he does.

DO YOU GO HOME?

violin   **vase**   **glove**

다음 단어의 빈 칸을 채우세요.

violin   vase   glove

v iolin   v ase   glo v e

◻ iolin   ◻ ase   glo ◻ e

V의 발음을 연구해 봅시다.

1. v[v]: 우리말에서 [ㅂ]로 발음됩니다.
   예 voice, vegetable, ………

2. v[v]: 우리말에서 [브]로 발음됩니다.
   예 valve, ………

NEW WORDS

go	come	**go**: 가다 **come**: 오다
walk	run	**walk**: 걷다 **run**: 뛰다
play	play tennis	**play**: 놀다 **play tennis**: 테니스를 치다

DO YOU GO HOME?

Do you go home?
Yes, I do.

Do you come home?
Yes, I come home.

Does he walk to school?
Yes, he does.

Does he run to school?
Yes, he runs to school.

Does she play tennis?
Yes, she does.

Does she play the violin?
Yes, she plays the violin.

★ 다음 <보기>처럼 의문문으로 만드세요.

 보기
You go home.
　　　Do you go home?
He goes home.
　　　Does he go home?

1. You walk to school.

2. He walks to school.

3. You play tennis.

4. He plays tennis.

5. You run to school.

★ 다음 문장을 해석하세요.

1. Do you go home?

   Yes, I do.

2. Does he walk to school?

   Yes, he does.

3. Does she play the violin?

   Yes, she plays the violin.

LESSON 23(TWENTY THREE)

DO YOU READ A BOOK?

water　　　**wolf**　　　**window**

다음 단어의 빈 칸을 채우세요.

water　　　　wolf　　　　window

|w| ater　　|w| olf　　windo |w|

|　| ater　　|　| olf　　windo |　|

W의 발음을 연구해 봅시다.

1. w[w]: 우리말에서 [우]로 발음됩니다.
   예 <u>w</u>eek, <u>w</u>e, <u>w</u>atch, ………

2. w[ ]: 우리말에서 발음되지 않습니다.
   예 <u>w</u>rite, <u>w</u>rong, ………

LESSON 23

NEW WORDS

read	write	**read**: 읽다 **write**: 쓰다
open	close	**open**: 열다 **close**: 닫다
get up	sleep	**get up**: 일어나 **sleep**: 자다

DO YOU READ A BOOK?

Do you read a book?
No, I don't.

Do you write a book?
No, I don't write a book.

Does he open the window?
No, he doesn't.

Does he close the window?
No, he doesn't close the window.

Does she get up at six?
No, she doesn't.

Does she sleep at ten?
No, she doesn't sleep at ten.

★ 다음 <보기>처럼 두 사람의 대화에서 _____친 곳에 알맞은 말을 써 넣으세요.

보기
Do you go to school?
　　Yes, I do.
Do you go to school?
　　No, I don't.

1. Do you go home?
　 Yes, I _____.

2. Do you go to school?
　 No, I _____.

3. Does he play tennis?
　 Yes, he _____.

4. Does he play the piano?
　 No, he _____.

5. Does she play the violin?
　 Yes, she _____.

★ 다음 문장을 해석하세요.

1. Does he go to school?
　 Yes, he does.

2. Does she get up at six?
　 Yes, she gets up at six.

3. Do you read a book?
　 No, I don't.

IT IS HOT TODAY.

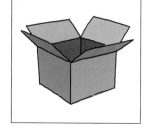

x-ray　　　**box**　　　**xylophone**

다음 단어의 빈 칸을 채우세요.

x-ray　　　　　box　　　　　xylophone

x -ray　　　　bo x 　　　　x ylophone

☐ -ray　　　　bo ☐ 　　　　☐ ylophone

X의 발음을 연구해 봅시다.

1. x[eks]: 우리말에서 [엑스]로 발음됩니다.

2. x[s]: 우리말에서 [스]로 발음됩니다.

3. x[z]: 우리말에서 [ㅈ]로 발음됩니다.

		hot: 더운 **cold**: 추운
hot	**cold**	
		fine: 좋은, 맑은 **cloudy**: 흐린
fine	**cloudy**	
		rainy: 비가 오는 **sunny**: 햇빛 나는
rainy	**sunny**	

IT IS HOT TODAY.

It is hot today.

It is cold today.

It is fine today.

It is cloudy today.

It is rainy today.

It is sunny today.

★ 다음 문장을 해석하세요.

1. It is hot today.

2. It is cold today.

3. It is fine today.

4. It is cloudy today.

5. It is rainy today.

★ 다음 단어의 뜻을 쓰세요.

1. bat :

2. glove :

3. doll :

4. toy car :

5. flute :

6. guitar :

7. go :

8. come :

9. walk :

10. run :

I AM STUDYING ENGLISH.

| yacht | baby | boy |

다음 단어의 빈 칸을 채우세요.

yacht   baby   boy

y acht   bab y   bo y

☐ acht   bab ☐   bo ☐

LESSON 25

Y의 발음을 연구해 봅시다.

1. y[y]: 우리말에서 [요]로 발음됩니다.

2. y[i]: 우리말에서 [이]로 발음됩니다.
   예 pretty, party, happy, ············· .

NEW WORDS

study	learn	**study**: 공부하다 **learn**: 배우다
listen	music	**listen**: 듣다 **music**: 음악
swim	river	**swim**: 수영하다 **river**: 강

I AM STUDYING ENGLISH.

I am studying English.

I am learning Korean.

You are listening to music.

You are playing baseball.

He is swimming in the river.

She is playing the piano.

★ 다음 <보기> 처럼 현재진행형으로 고치세요.

 I play baseball.
　　　　 I am playing baseball.

1. I study English.

2. I learn Korean.

3. You listen to music.

4. You play basketball.

5. He swims in the river.

6. She plays the piano.

7. I read a book.

8. He reads a book.

9. She opens the window.

10. You open the window.

STAND UP, PLEASE.

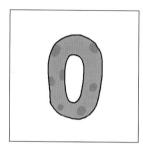

zoo   **zero**   **zebra**

다음 단어의 빈 칸을 채우세요.

zoo   zero   zebra

| z | oo | z | ero | z | ebra

| | oo | | ero | | ebra

Z의 발음을 연구해 봅시다.

1. z[z]: 우리말에서 [즈]로 발음됩니다.
   예 zeal, zealous, zigzag, ············

NEW WORDS

stand up	**sit down**	**stand up**: 일어나다 **sit down**: 앉다
come in	**go out**	**come in**: 들어오다 **go out**: 나가다
drink	**water**	**drink**: 마시다 **water**: 물

STAND UP, PLEASE.

Stand up, please.

Sit down, please.

Please come in.

Please go out.

Let's drink water.

Let's play baseball.

 ★ 다음 <보기>처럼 명령문을 만드세요.

> **보기**
> You stand up.
> Stand up, please.
> Please stand up.

1. You sit down.

2. You come in.

3. You go out.

★ 다음 문장을 해석하세요.

1. I learn Korean.

2. I am learning Korean.

3. He swims in the river.

4. He is swimming in the river.

5. Stand up, please.

6. Please come in.

7. Let's play baseball.